Butler School

Rob Waring, *Series Editor*

HEINLE
CENGAGE Learning

Australia • Brazil • Japan • Korea • Mexico • Singapore • Spain • United Kingdom • United States

Words to Know

This story is set in the country of England, which is in the United Kingdom.

ENGLAND

EUROPE

N
W E
S

 A Land of Tradition. Read the paragraph. Then match each word or phrase with the correct definition.

In the past, it was popular for rich ladies and gentlemen in England to have large country houses. They often had servants to help with the cooking and cleaning. Servants are not as common today, but many people still consider butlers to be very important. They usually manage most of the duties around the home. Kings and queens still have servants, though, a palace is a very big place to run!

1. lady _____	**a.** the large home of a king or queen
	b. a person who runs a home as a job
2. gentleman _____	**c.** an older term for a woman of high social position
3. country house _____	**d.** a large house outside of the city
4. servant _____	**e.** an older term for a man of high social position
5. butler _____	**f.** a general term for someone who works and lives in someone else's house doing housework
6. palace _____	

B **A School for Butlers.** Read the paragraph. Then complete the definitions with the correct form of the word.

The Ivor Spencer [ivər spɛnsər] International School for Butler Administrators teaches people how to be butlers. At the school, students learn special phrases and titles, such as 'Sir' or 'Madam.' At the end of the course, successful students graduate. They get certificates that say they are ready to work as a butler. Their employers are often important people, such as lords, or people who represent their nation internationally, such as ambassadors.

1. An official document that shows that something is true is a c_____.

2. To complete one's education successfully is to g_____.

3. A word such as 'Mr.' or 'Dr.' before a name is a t_____.

4. L_____ is a British term for a man of high social class.

5. Government members that officially represent their country in another country are a_____.

country house

lady

gentleman

servants

An English Country House

In the past, England was a land of beautiful old country houses, palaces, gardens, and afternoon tea. It was also a country where every real gentleman had servants, especially a butler. Now, things have changed. Just 70 years ago, there were tens of thousands of butlers in England; now there are only a few. So in modern England, where does one find a good butler? More importantly, where does one learn how to become one?

 CD 1, Track 09

They study at the Ivor Spencer International School for Butler Administrators—of course! The Ivor Spencer School is on the grounds of a beautiful country house. It specializes in teaching men and women how to be butlers.

It's the first day of class and the students are learning how to properly introduce themselves to their employer, or their 'gentleman' or 'lady.' This is a very important skill for butlers and must be done in the correct way.

The students practice introducing themselves to one of the teachers. "Good evening, sir. My name is Michael. I'm your butler," says one student perfectly. "My name is Jose," says another. Another repeats, "I'm your butler," until he gets it just right. One student even moves on to offering his imaginary employer food and drink: "Can I bring you some **refreshments**,[1] sir?" he says seriously. Unfortunately, some students have trouble. One student can't stop laughing as he says "Good evening, sir." A good butler should never laugh while talking to his or her employer!

---

[1]**refreshments:** food and drinks

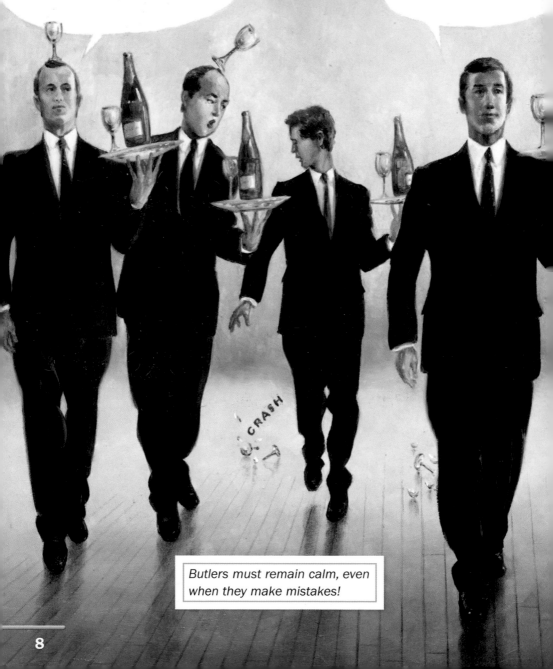

Butlers must remain calm, even when they make mistakes!

A proper butler must also **carry himself**[2] correctly. At the Ivor Spencer School, the future butlers must learn how to walk with a completely straight back. What's the best way to learn how to do this? Students put glasses on their heads and walk. If their heads and backs aren't completely straight, the glasses won't be either, and you know what that means—crash!

The group slowly moves across the floor. They are carefully carrying trays of **champagne**[3] and practicing the phrase, "Your champagne, my lady." As they continue walking, you can hear the sound of glasses crashing to the floor. It looks like these students need more practice! Of course, good butlers must also remain calm, even when they make mistakes. To practice this, the students repeat "No problem, sir," as the glasses continue to drop around them.

---

[2] **carry (oneself):** move one's body in a particular way
[3] **champagne:** a special, bubbly, and usually expensive kind of wine

These days, if you ask an average English person about butlers, they say things like: "Butlers? I haven't seen a butler for a long time." It's true that there aren't many butlers in England these days. Seventy years ago, there were an estimated thirty thousand butlers. Today there are fewer than 200. But if Ivor Spencer has anything to say about it, that's going to change!

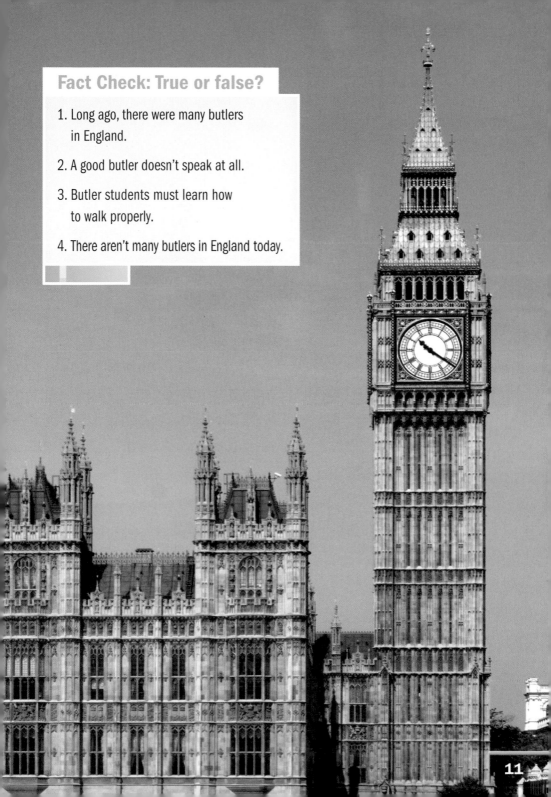

Fact Check: True or false?

1. Long ago, there were many butlers in England.

2. A good butler doesn't speak at all.

3. Butler students must learn how to walk properly.

4. There aren't many butlers in England today.

Ivor Spencer wants to use his school to bring back the butler to this land of tradition. He wants to teach people how to be **polite**[4] and proper English butlers.

Mr. Spencer is very pleased with each new group of young men and women who come to learn at his school. "Good morning, everybody," he says to his new students, "Welcome to the Ivor Spencer School. We know you've come from all over the world and we **appreciate**[5] your being here." Then the hard work begins.

---

[4]**polite:** acting in a kind and proper way
[5]**appreciate:** be thankful for

Future butlers must learn many important things. One of the most important things is how to refer to employers, guests, and visitors correctly. Many of these people are very important, and there are several different titles that can be used. Butlers should say, "Good morning, Your Excellency," when they are talking to ambassadors or certain rulers. However, they must use 'Your Highness' when talking to a king or queen. In addition, there are still other titles, such as 'Your Grace' for lords and other important people. There are so many names to learn!

Over the next five weeks, 13 students from countries such as Spain and Canada will have 86 lessons in the art of being a butler. If they succeed, they may work for a rich businessman, an important leader, or even a king some day. However, first, they have to graduate—and that's not easy. The Ivor Spencer International School for Butler Administrators is basically a **training camp**[6] for butlers!

---

[6]**training camp:** a serious and difficult place where competitors or fighters go to learn their skills

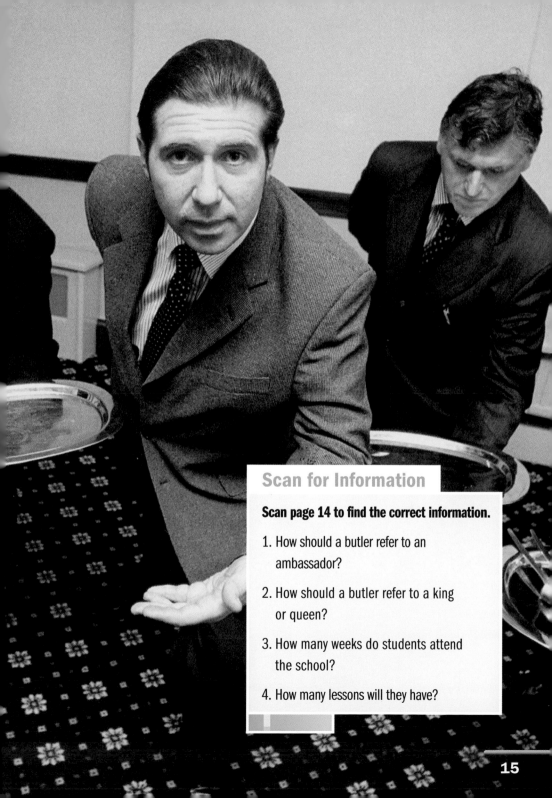

Scan for Information

Scan page 14 to find the correct information.

1. How should a butler refer to an ambassador?

2. How should a butler refer to a king or queen?

3. How many weeks do students attend the school?

4. How many lessons will they have?

Mr. Spencer talks about how difficult the training is at his school. He says that some people can't even last longer than the first few days. "On every course there are about two people that don't make it past the first two days," he reports. This may come true for one student in the new group, **David Marceau**.[7] He's having trouble saying the correct phrases for answering the telephone. He doesn't mind Mr. Spencer's corrections, though. "**Practice makes perfect**,"[8] says David, "so hopefully, with a lot of practice, I'll be just as good as any other butler out there."

It's very difficult to become a good butler. It's much harder than people think it is. That's why it's important for students to **keep their hopes up**[9] and to keep trying. One student says, "I just hope I'm going to be right for the job and hope I can do it." It seems that one way to be sure is to practice, practice, practice!

---

[7] **David Marceau:** [deɪvɪd mɑrsou]
[8] **practice makes perfect:** a saying that means 'if you work hard, you will improve'
[9] **keep (one's) hopes up:** maintain a positive or good attitude

Butlers must often carry food and drinks at their job. In fact, the word 'butler' comes from the French word *bouteiller*, which means 'person who carries a bottle.' For a new butler, carrying a bottle can be very difficult. They must walk with a very straight back, keep their eyes ahead and carry the bottle carefully. It takes a lot of concentration and practice; the students are soon practicing again. They're walking around the room with glasses on their heads, trays in their hands, and smiles on their faces. As they walk, the future butlers repeat the same phrases:

"It's a pleasure, sir."
"No problem, sir."
"Your champagne, my lord."
"I'll **fetch**[10] it immediately, sir."
"Good evening, sir."

Things go better for everyone this time. Very few glasses are dropped. It seems that all the practice is showing some results! Even David Marceau is showing improvement. As he **proudly**[11] repeats, "Your champagne, my lady," his glass stays securely on his head.

---

[10]**fetch (something):** go and get (something)
[11]**proud:** pleased or satisfied with something that one has achieved

By the third week of the course, the students start to find out if they really can become butlers or not. David is having trouble with the proper phrases again. The words just won't come out right! "It's very difficult here," he says. "It's very difficult. The course isn't easy at all." He might be nervous, but he also knows that he can improve. "I have some problems, and I have to deal with them," he says.

David is not just having difficulty with the course, he also misses his friends and family back home. "I miss my girlfriend very much," he says. "She's giving me support on the phone. I just talked to her last night. Things are okay and everything … I wish I were there right now."

As the course progresses, the students move on from the basic exercises to the 'higher arts,' or the more specialized parts of the job. There are a lot of secrets to being a good butler who gets everything just right. For example, did you know that you can **iron**[12] a newspaper to make it look nice and avoid leaving **ink**[13] everywhere? Ivor Spencer does, and he teaches the class how to do it.

"That's probably the only time the butler has to read the newspaper," Mr. Spencer explains to the group. "If you see a burnt newspaper, you know the butler's been very interested," he says with a laugh. The class enjoys the fun, but then it's back to serious work!

---

[12] **iron:** use a special hot tool called an 'iron' to make cloth smooth
[13] **ink:** a colored material that is used for writing, printing, or drawing

Choosing a Pipe

Defending the House

Selecting the Wine

The Higher Arts of Being a Butler

24

Sometimes butlers need other unusual skills. For example, they might need to deal with unwelcome guests. They may have to stop someone who tries to get into the house to take things. These butlers will be ready. The Ivor Spencer School even teaches them how to protect themselves and their households with a champagne bottle!

Butlers must also learn how to recognize good quality products, or 'the finer things in life.' To learn more about this, the students go out to different stores. "It's not a piece of wood. It is a piece of art," explains one shop owner as he teaches the students about **tobacco pipes**.[14] They are also shown around an expensive shoe store. Then finally, of course, they learn about the best champagne.

---

[14]**tobacco pipe:** a tube with a bowl-shaped part that is used to smoke a special kind of dried leaves

At last, graduation day arrives. Everyone is very happy to be finished with their training and they're very proud to receive their certificates—especially David Marceau. After a lot of hard work, he's made it! "David, you've come a long way," says Mr. Spencer as he hands David his certificate.

After the graduation, the students have a small party—complete with champagne. "I did it!" says one very happy student. "To good health," says Mr. Spencer. Before they came here, these young men and women may have driven buses, worked with computers, or even worked in restaurants or stores. Now, they are butlers and they are part of a very old English tradition. The Ivor Spencer International School for Butler Administrators has done its job well!

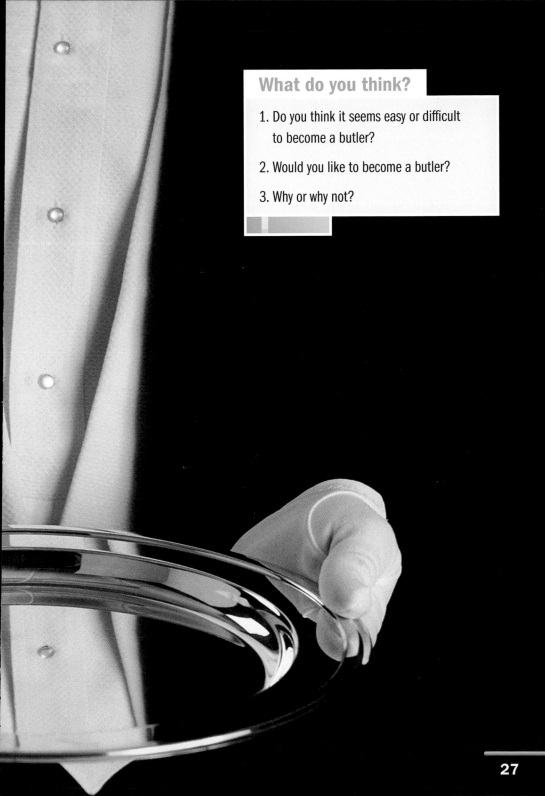

What do you think?

1. Do you think it seems easy or difficult to become a butler?

2. Would you like to become a butler?

3. Why or why not?

After You Read

1. On page 5, the word 'real' can be replaced by:
   A. rich
   B. possible
   C. proper
   D. legal

2. Which of the following is a good heading for page 5?
   A. Butlers Still Common in Country Houses
   B. Butlers Less Popular but Still Present
   C. A Thousand-Year-Old Tradition
   D. Modern Butlers Not Good Enough

3. In paragraph 3 on page 6, what mistake does one student make when practicing his introduction?
   A. He laughs.
   B. He asks for refreshments.
   C. He forgets his name.
   D. He doesn't say 'sir.'

4. A butler learns to walk straight _____ a glass on his head.
   A. while
   B. by
   C. because
   D. with

5. What does Ivor Spencer think about butlers in England?
   A. He hasn't seen one for a long time.
   B. He thinks they are useless.
   C. He believes there should be more.
   D. He thinks no one should be a butler.

6. Which of the following people might have a butler?
   A. a tourist in England
   B. a leader of a country
   C. a school teacher
   D. a servant

7. Which of the following is a good heading for page 17?
   A. All the Butlers Will Graduate
   B. Butler School Not So Difficult
   C. Some Students Will Leave Early
   D. Ivor Doesn't Like Students

8. In paragraph 1 on page 18, 'it' in the phrase 'it takes a lot of concentration' refers to:
   A. carrying a champagne tray
   B. being a student
   C. carrying a glass
   D. walking

9. On page 21, how is David Marceau feeling?
   A. He plans to leave the school.
   B. He misses his regular life.
   C. He is not sure he wants to be a butler.
   D. He has no hope.

10. In paragraph 2 on page 25, the word 'recognize' can be replaced by:
   A. identify
   B. see
   C. experience
   D. discover

11. Why do butlers also have to know about the finer things in life?
   A. because they must know how to protect the household
   B. because they must pretend to be rich
   C. because they will become rich working as a butler
   D. because their employers will need good products

12. What's the main idea of paragraph 2 on page 26?
   A. The students are starting a new life thanks to their training.
   B. Being a butler is better than other jobs.
   C. Foreigners cannot join this English tradition.
   D. Both men and women can be modern butlers.

The Butler Always Knows Best!

A Short Story
by John Clayburg

Although the Finches were extremely rich, they were very relaxed. The only way people knew that they were rich was because of their beautiful house and their long-time butler. "James was here when we bought the house," Lord Finch always said. "We can't live without him now. He always knows best!"

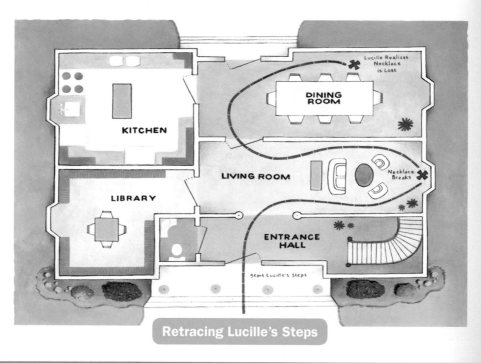

Retracing Lucille's Steps

One day, Lord and Lady Finch were having a party at their country house. They invited their neighbors, Ambassador Raynor and his wife Lucille, for dinner. First, everyone met in the entrance hall. Then, James served everyone a glass of champagne in the living room. There, Lucille and Lady Finch stopped at the window to enjoy the view of the garden. Afterwards, they moved to the dining room to sit down for dinner.

Suddenly, halfway through the meal, the ambassador's wife cried, "Oh dear! Something terrible has happened. I've lost my necklace!" "Don't worry. We'll find it!" said Lord Finch. "James can fix anything. James?" Lord Finch called to the butler. James entered the dining room and turned to Lucille. "What kind of necklace is it?" he asked. "Oh a very special one," she said. "It was given to my grandmother by Queen Victoria." After that James quietly walked out of the room.

Lucille was terribly disappointed with James, but then five minutes later, he returned with the necklace. The people in the room reacted with surprise. He then explained how he did it. "It was actually quite easy, my lord," he said calmly. "Madam Raynor mentioned that the necklace was received from Queen Victoria. So, I realized that it was very old. Old necklaces can break very easily. It was easy to guess that the necklace fell off somewhere. I only had to find out where it happened. So, I simply followed her steps for the day."

He then carefully handed the necklace back to Lucille and said, "Will that be all, Madam?" The woman took the necklace and said, "Thank you so very much, James!" "You're welcome, Madam," said James as he calmly went back to work. "See?" cried Lord Finch, "I told you! The butler always knows best!"

CD 1, Track 10

Word Count: 352
Time: _____

Vocabulary List

ambassador (3, 14, 15)
appreciate (13)
butler (2, 3, 5, 6, 8, 9, 10, 11, 13, 14, 15, 17, 18, 21, 22, 24, 25, 26, 27)
carry (oneself) (9)
certificate (3, 26)
champagne (8, 9, 18, 25, 26)
country house (2, 3, 5, 6)
fetch (18)
gentleman (2, 3, 5, 6)
graduate (3, 14, 26)
ink (22)
iron (22)
keep (one's) hopes up (17)
lady (2, 3, 6, 8, 9, 18)
lord (3, 14, 18)
palace (2, 5)
polite (13)
practice makes perfect (17)
proud (18, 26)
refreshment (6)
servant (2, 3, 5)
title (3, 14)
tobacco pipe (25)
training camp (14)